BY THE LIGHT OF A NEON MOON

Poetry out of dancehalls, honky tonks, music halls, and clubs

edited by Janet Lowery

MADVILLE
PUBLISHING

Lake Dallas, Texas

FIRST EDITION

Requests for permission to reprint or reuse material from this work should be sent to:

Permissions
Madville Publishing
PO Box 358
Lake Dallas, TX 75065

Acknowledgements:
The following poems are reprinted from earlier publications with the authors' permission.

- "A Thing About Rhumba" by Gianna Russo, reprinted from *Moonflower* (Kitsune Books, 2011)
- "Road House on the Way to Cheyenne" by Rick Campbell, reprinted from *The Traveler's Companion* (Black Bay Books, 2004)
- "Oh, That Buckskin" by Chrisitine Cock, reprinted from *The Mosaic III* (2017)
- "The Bull Rider" and "Prickly Pear" by Katherine Hoerth, reprinted from *Goddess Wears Cowboy Boots* (Lamar, 2014)
- "Zydeco Shindig" by Dolores Comeaux, reprinted from *A Collection by AZ Writers*
- "Little Heretic" by Gerry LaFemina, reprinted from *Little Heretic* (Stephen F. Austin UP, 2014)
- "Empties" by Gerry LaFemina, reprinted from *Graffiti Heart* (Mammoth Books, 2003)
- "Waiting for Resurrection" by Leah Mueller, previously published by Outlaw Poetry (Online)
- "Integration 1964" and "Two Dogs Howling at the Moon" by Dave Parsons, reprinted from *Feathering Deep* (Texas Review Press, 2011)
- "Music for Arms Like Ours" by Mike Schneider, reprinted from *Mainstreet Rag* (Summer 2004)
- "Friday's Dance" by Mike Schneider, reprinted from *Antietam Review*

Cover Design: Jacqueline Davis
Cover Image: Austin, Texas - June 13, 2014, Peek Creative Collective / Shutterstock.com

ISBN: 978-1-948692-12-0 paper, and 978-1-948692-13-7 ebook
Library of Congress Control Number: 2018968038

Contents

II—Neon Signs

III—Neon Hearts

Introduction

The subject of the poems collected in *By the Light of a Neon Moon* could hardly be called "elevated," but if, as Philip Larkin noted and Kim Davis quoted in her submissions-call for this anthology, "poetry preserves the memory of the human race," the poetry collected here memorializes the atmosphere and character of dancehalls, honky tonks, clubs, and music halls, where (mainly) country western music is played, sung, or spun; where patrons dance, listen, and watch couples dance, in particular, the Two-Step, Polka, Shuffle, and Waltz. I am happy to note that three Texas State Poet Laureates are included in this collection: Alan Birkelbach, karla k. morton, and Dave Parsons, lending it an authentic Texas tenor. Also represented on these pages are prize-winning poets such as Carolyn Kreiter-Foronda, Poet Laureate of the state of Virginia 2006-2008, Gerry LaFemina, winner of the Anthony Piccione Poetry Award from Mammoth Press, George Drew, winner of the X. J. Kennedy Award from Texas Review Press, Gianna Russo, winner of a Florida Book Award for her collection *Moonflower*, various members of the Texas Institute of Letters, including Jerry Bradley and Katherine Hoerth—also winner of the Helen C. Smith Prize for poetry—as well as many other notable poets.

Although a few other types of clubs and genres of music or dance are represented on these pages (see Gianna Russo's "A Thing About Rhumba" for a Latin twist, Dolores Comeaux's "Zydeco Shindig" for some Cajun fare, and Gerry LaFemina's "Little Heretic," "Guitar and Mandolin," and "Empties" for punk rock or blues references), this collection celebrates, in particular, the culture of country western dance (a brand of regional folk-dance, right?) found in cities like Houston, Dallas, Austin, San Antonio, most small towns in Texas, and in regions surrounding the Lone Star State.

I come to this subject by way of the vibrant dance subculture in

Houston, but my interest here is in preserving that dance culture and its character in poetry, a culture that is "hanging on by a thread," to quote Damon D'Amico, one of the foremost dance instructors in Houston. He defines a country western nightclub as a "watering hole for people of the community, a place to put down differences and drink from the same pond, a place where moms and dads go for good clean fun and to which they introduce their kids when it's time, a place where young and old alike hang out together for a good time." Unlike other kinds of music clubs that come and go as fads in music enter then exit popular culture, country western nightclubs are an "American tradition," he says. Dancers in Houston have DJs like Brad Turney to thank for keeping danceable music spinning in the dancehalls; in other towns, country bands keep dancers' feet boot-scooting across the wooden floors.

As for country music—I need hardly defend a tradition that Gram Parsons defined as "the purest form of American music," and "Cosmic American Music." I hope the poetry collected here inspires you to visit a local country western nightclub, enjoy the music and dancing, and two-step your way into more fun than you can imagine (after some practice)!

—*Janet Lowery*
November, 2018

I

Neon Light

Beloved, After These Things

Alan Birkelbach

If three dances in
on the crowded wooden floor
he keeps coming back to you
and you still have not been bruised
by an errant elbow,
or had to wonder where his lead was,
then it's time to look him
right there in the center of the pool of his eyes.
But don't say a word.
Just make sure
there's a far-off ache there,
a yearning for a saddle,
lots of long, rainy nights,
bad campfire coffee,
something as strong and dependable
as wooden rails and leather gloves.
Admit to yourself you're second.
You'll always be second.
He's in love with the moon
and arroyos and thunder.
You'll want to teach him to take risks.
You'll know he already knows how.

Like People in Love

Kimberly Parish Davis

They swirled and danced
two-stepping in the dust
of cow dung long since
carried on the wind.
Pointy-toed cowboy boots
swinging out behind one
then the other. I'd
never seen them dance
before, and I never did again.
I sprawled across two
chairs pushed together,
a Shirley Temple
by my head.
I watched the boots
slide by, too fast,
their familiar grace—
like people in love—
swirled out of sight,
replaced by strangers.

A Thing About Rhumba

Gianna Russo

It was the 42nd year of my undulations
it was night spilling south out of borealis
the stars all frazzled
it was the second year of our second marriage
the days of naked lavender and blue slumber
it was our first year of dancing in public
the itchy moodiness of chairs around a floor
the broody nudgings of a microphone
it was a Latin trio
the interior sultriness of rhumba
it was a Morse code calling from your pulse to mine
the slight caesura of your lead
the way desire spun between us
it was the suggestion of port on your lips
it was the joke of martinis
it was the saltiness of the saxophone signed by your palm
there, at the small of my back
it was the swollen voice of the conga
it was candlelight spurning the shadows
the still-warm steps that stumbled out of doors
it was the awning clearing the constellations
the precise way we mapped the darkness of Hyde Park
the way silence navigated the street
until from an upstairs window
shutters thrown wide to night air
the curtains dazed with moonlight
it was his low needful grunting
his grunting and her moans
her question-and-answer moans
her moans like interpreters of longing
it was their cries signaling the still-point
they came to

coming beside the open window
coming beside themselves
it was you and I
it was breath and silver
holding on, listening.

PRETTY WOMAN

Luanne Smith

For Judy J.

I

Jay is Kim Basinger with a little
Daryl Hannah mixed in. Curly
hair she hates that never looks
as bad as she thinks. One night,
in a basement bar, shapely legs
in jeans and cowboy boots appear
on the steps outside. A male friend
actually leered. "I'd recognize those
legs anywhere." I never told Jay this.
It doesn't matter. She pushes away
advances like running through rain
with an umbrella. Not a drop of such
smooth talk touches her. She is so
used to this kind of thing.

II

In Austin visiting Jay, I get my first
tattoo, following Jay's lead, though
hers is a colorful hummingbird on
the ankle and mine is a simple
line drawing of a heron, same
ankle. Maybe, Jay is why
I have so many tattoos now.
Months before, after we went
into Philly for her tattoo, she left
Pennsylvania, a job she'd grown
tired of, a man she'd chosen with
wiry Where's Waldo looks who
surprised us all with his abuse.

III

But I miss her. When a friend throws
you a birthday party outside where you
all toss emptied champagne bottles
over your shoulders while the next
is being opened . . . that's a friend you
miss. In Austin, visiting, I eat a mountain
of barbecue, Mexican food
for breakfast and go to roadside
bars with her for beer in small juice
glasses, Spanish whirling all around us.

IV

We go to The Broken Spoke,
a famous honky tonk, though
I had no idea honky tonks
could be famous. I watch her
slice her way right into the room,
the crowd, the men, this New Yorker,
transplanted to Pennsylvania,
transplanted to Texas. I grew up
in Kentucky, and I stand there wondering,
where did Jay learn to two step like that?

V

I am clumsy on the dance floor, in spite
of Kentucky deep inside me. I don't
twirl well. I don't own cowboy
boots made to scoot these days, I am
horrible at letting the man lead. Dancing
backwards makes me dizzy. I step
aside, more embarrassed than I
should be. No one is paying any attention
to me. A Shiner Bock and Kamikazi shot.

Jay glides in a circle on the floor,
turning, polite to this cowboy
who doesn't have a chance.

VI

I switch to Kentucky Bourbon. I am
the one who knows every word
to Hank Williams, Jerry Lee Lewis,
Vince Gill, Roy Orbison, Dwight Yoakam.
The throaty lead singer lacks the proper
high pitch for these vocals, the proper
twang. I'm the one who knows
the guys in the band spread sand on plywood
at their feet, put a mike
on it, and slip their boots across
for a scratchy, old record sound.

VII

I am the one sitting at the table
off to the side, watching my best
friend taking over this world. Her
signature laugh reaches my ears
over sand and song, chatter
and bottle clinks. I switch to Maker's
Mark, like I have the money, and
I wish silently for the band to play
Dwight Yoakam's "A Thousand Miles
From Nowhere," a favorite
of mine, to take me away from The
Broken Spoke, from Austin, from
my pretty woman friend who
was leaving me behind before
we even knew each other.

Not That Sally

George Drew

Not that Sally, not Mustang Sally, but the Sally
I remember was long and tall and did have legs
that loved to dance the summer nights away

on small dance floors in bars, the bubbly Sally
with her Joisey accent and her Joisey ways;

that Sally, the girl with shapely alabaster legs,
dancer's legs that never knew a dance they
didn't like, twist or stroll or mashed potatoes;

the girl Skeeter B fell for, shadowdancing her
into the one who didn't get away, dream girl
who danced so hard the floorboards groaned.

The Sally I remember is the one I met days
after Skeeter's sister, my first wife, died
when I stopped by her grave to grieve

and when I asked what she was doing there
replied with flowers in a jar and a sad smile.

That Sally I remember, not Mustang Sally,
but the Joisey girl with flashing feet,
the girl the summer nights begged for mercy.

Dear Will's Pub

Pj Metz

All my potential energy rests
in the measures between songs wrenched
from the heart of a steaming bar on Mills Ave,
20 miles from a Magic Kingdom,
An hour and a half from saltwater that rusts cars and brains,
And lightyears from
work.

It's atomic upon release, focused and brighter
than the flash of stage lights off guitar pegs
angrier than the snap of a broken stick
great crackling walls of sound careen off floors
sticky with blue ribbon and walls covered with
stickers of bands who made their mark
at least once.

It's been years of music, near two decades;
I'm not sure what the half-life of a punk cd
or a patched-up denim vest is,
whether I'll still be putting in earplugs
and dancing in a circle
and holding my drink high so the singer knows
I hear you, we hear you, sing louder, scream
so Florida will sink
so Orlando will rise
so we can collide at the speed of light and
Burn.

I'm not sure how long it'll be till
smoke clears till
vegetation eats the stage till
another damn fusion restaurant takes its place
but
I'm not as worried as you would think

about losing the glow and sound
because
the only thing true about nights like these
is that they'll never end.
I've drank Asahi in Tokyo,
Swilled soju in seven cities of Korea,
Chased beer with beer around Oceania,
But
Nothing will ever fill me like riffs
from whoever is on stage at Will's Pub.

Rose-Colored

Janet Lowery

free class at the dancehall

At the fixed hour for class,
his new crush fails to show up.
One heart-chamber clenches shut
then rattles against the Gordian knot
that guards its gate. Breath stalled,
fluids in his knees slosh and almost
buckle beneath his sagging weight.
His shuffle step misses a beat.
Breathe, he commands, then pushes
disappointment into his boot-heals.
He picks up the two-step count
and reminds himself the come-and-go
of young follows is ruled by the moon.

Slow to crank his classmate into
her double turn, slow to sail her off
into a free spin, he picks her up again
a half-beat late; the instructor
catches his eye in rebuke—he's the lead,
an old-timer, the one who must rock
steady for the woman following him.
He's supposed to count with his feet—
not his tin-heart. Muscle-memory
kicks in; he rights the course they travel;
dancers bend time with their minds,
mend a broken pace with a quick-
quick, quick-quick, quick-step turn.

At the one-hour mark, class ends,
partners step apart and the real rodeo begins.
Lights dim and social dancers couple up.
Drinkers line the rails to watch

pleated skirts flare along the line of dance.
Our hero waits for the downbeat
to hit his feet, for some old friend,
a former flame to grab his hand
and pull him onto the floor. No point
in sitting out a song for the no-show—
a dance in place progresses nowhere;
buried in the bed of his hand lost minutes
stall time forever. To hell with that.

In sync with fiddle, banjo, mandolin,
he wonders if there's still time to find a girl,
one who won't wax and wane untrue,
play him for a fool—but wait—he's the fool;
he's never said a word to her about the way
his heart bucks crazy inside his chest
when she smiles at him. He looks out
at the wide open spaces of the honky-tonk
dance floor—his refuge from the mundane,
the ordinary, the civilian platform he paces
everyday on his way to get here. He prays
to the muse of dance for another chance
to pitch woo to the girl who smiles at him,

but he feels lost. The deejay spins a waltz
sung by a man adorned with glasses the color
of roses to keep from seeing the truth
about women and losses. The melancholy
romances his heart, sparks love-sickness—
as if from out the incorporeal air, a dark
Cupid flew into the hall, fully armed to tighten
our hero's heart-knot, reboot his gloom,
inspire rosy nostalgia for what might have been.
He grabs his old flame's hand, the love he dumped
a month ago. On cue, the new girl strolls in
on the arm of another man. Close call, he thinks,
and circle turns his partner around the room.

Old Flame

Winston Derden

Nothing but the jukebox
on a slow Wednesday night,
Merle and Tammy, Patsy and Hank
singing songs of another time.

Same old couples turning
'round and 'round, unjostled
by the rowdy weekend crowd,
unflustered by a band playing loud.

No money made on a night like this,
a few coffees or Cokes, fewer beers,
but there are the regulars
who always trickle in,

families with young ones learning
time-told steps from older sister
or taking turns with mom and dad,

but I keep the lights on
to see the old couples dance
step by step, affirming romance.

Two in particular in the corner of my eye,
old when they started, years gone by,
they never miss a Wednesday night.

Every week, they close the evening out
waltzing, fingertip to fingertip,
barely touching, intimately in touch.

From the first I saw them,
I believed in love.

Music for Arms Like Ours

Mike Schneider

Splash of voodoo water
& three grinds of Jamaican pepper
so I'll be good to munch on, cooked
or raw & next thing
I'm shuffling to saxophone blues
with Rebecca, beautiful, like fire
or sunset or white Nicaraguan rum
with lemons you shake from a tree at twilight
while Carl Sandburg sings about old horses
& it makes you cry, because time is running
away. No real woman can be this lovely
I'm thinking & then the band breaks
to wipe sweat. Then restarts, fate
having unloosed Alyssa, lanky
as I slide in close, that tango
lean I learned, her smile
of Welcome Stranger, step right up
& I don't know how to hide
that I want her more than watermelon
in July, how it heals thirst, eyes
glittering like black seeds
I'd draw into my mouth
& spit them at my cousins & laugh
& run fast until the room turns
& she's gone & I'm rewinding myself
like a stopped clock when time is ripe
to dance like this. Music for arms
like ours to reach for each other
& hold on swirling like feathers of snow
in moonlight, lighter even than that. Eyes
closed, all the long nights, lifetimes
you wait to be alive like Mickey Rooney
and Judy Garland, one of those hey
gang, let's do a show, let's sing & dance

the rest of our lives. We can do it
if we want to, we could dance & sing
the rest of our lives. We could.

Oh, That Buckskin

Christine Cock

How did they do it?
How did audiences, episode after episode
accept the greatest love story never told.

> He, larger than life, voice calmer than still water,
> and a flame-haired beauty, owner of the only
> *respectable* boarding house/saloon

in the entire West. Ever. Matt Dillon had no history,
never wavered when fighting for fairness, truth
and justice for Dodge City. While Miss Kitty,

> curvaceously high-collared, offered hard-luck
> strangers free meals, steered wayward women
> from dangerous liaisons,

kept firm hold over ruffians cheating at cards
or itching to throw a punch. When the Marshall was called
into hinterlands, she leaned on a porch column,

> watched him throw his leg over
> that massive buckskin's flank, then trot
> down bustling Main Street with no more than a tip

of the Stetson's stiff brim and searing backward glance.
Soon, (music changes tempo), Doc's worried brow,
and the red-head drumming her nails on the table

> concerned us all. Town citizens held their breath.
> Matt returned, tilting in the saddle, prisoner tied
> to some paint horse's pommel. Doc dug out the bullet,

wrapped Matt's shoulder wound while our matronly
Miss Kitty patted his hand, quipped about getting
back to work, then admonished twittering Festus just because.

      Oh, if only I had been that lovely Madam the moment
      saloon doors swung open revealing Mr. Dillon's rugged silhouette
      blocking the setting sun! Once road dust was kicked

off boots, hat slapped on stained, road-worn pants,
I'd have run to him, slipped my hand into his firm grip,
and led him up the staircase.

      At the landing, I'd have stopped,
      leaned over the wooden balustrade, signaling
      Barkeep to continue sliding mugs

down the shining copper top. Then, with a nod
toward the piano player that said,
"pound those ivories hard tonight,"

      Matt and I would have turned toward each other
      with slow, wicked grins, knowing no raucous dance hall stomper

could hear my marshal's gun belt as it clattered onto the floor.

Dancing Fool

John Grey

So that's what it's about, the dancing,
even though I can't dance,
put the world at risk with my three left feet
and helicopter arms.
She says she feels the need for romance
and only dancing fits her bill.
But I should wear a sign,
a "Beware Of The Dog" for waltzers.
There should be posters of me
in every dance hall in the country
warning "Stop the music on sight."
She likes to tell me it's the thought that counts.
But it counts 1-2-3, 1-2-3.
Only not in that order.

Always Open

Karen Head

In the dream, I'm back on the road
driving south from Lincoln, NE
toward Kansas City, windows half way
down, Midwest winter air smacking me
awake, reminding me to breathe.
I'm suffering.
Homesickness is the story
I tell, but I know there's more to it,
this loneliness, these too fast
heartbeats, this need to escape.

Just outside St. Joe, traffic
from the KC aiport roars
overhead, and just off the exit
I see it, glowing warm yellow
in the darkness, so I pull in.
This is no photoshopped Hopper
Nighthawks. No, this is home,
always open, always there
waiting for me past any curfew.

I shake snow from my hair,
find the place empty, except for
one counter stool, which begins
to spin and Bourdain tells me to
join him, so I do because
I've got nowhere else to be.
I shout, "scattered, smothered,
covered, diced, and capped,"
and laughter erupts. Now the place
is full of people I couldn't save.
We are all eating pecan waffles,
telling each other stories, and I say,
"Someday, maybe, I'll find a way to be happy,"

and Bourdain says, "Don't you have
somewhere you should be?"
The faint sound of the airplanes
begins to amplify, everything begins to shake.
I dive down, cover my ears,
shut my eyes to the looming shadows—

startled, I find myself back in Atlanta,
you are snoring again,
and, for once, for always, this makes me happy.

WORDS FROM MY FATHER

karla k. morton

—*Pete Martin's School of Dance*

Let him lead you.
Stay up on your toes
so you can move easily
with his body.

Let his summer wind
whisk you around and around
till you're giddy with dizzy,
too busy to foresee
tomorrow.

Trust him—backwards, blind.
Lean forward on a man
whose shoulders can hold you,
whose body yangs to your ying,
who makes you wake up singing.

We know you can open your own doors.
Hell, you could lead if you wanted,
but chivalry is a gift
the woman gives the man
to make us feel strong, wanted, needed;
perhaps a bit invincible.

Tomorrow will be what tomorrow always is—
but on that dance floor,
he is yours
and you are his,
and for three to five minutes,
this world is as perfect
as this world ever gets.

ONE WAY TRAFFIC

Alan Birkelbach

A real short verse of deep regret.
A girl he saw but didn't get.
His steps were good but she let go.
He tried to dance against the flow.

Dancing at Dirty Frank's

Lisa Naomi Konigsberg

for Charles L. Armour

Holes in the wood paneling from darts
that missed their mark, drunks leaning
like fallen angels against the jukebox, and
sparks flying off of cigarettes like tiny
unannounced fireworks.
"Play Smokey Robinson—or something smooth—shit,
we need a good groove up in here!"
"Oooo, baby, baby.
Oooo, baby, baby.
I'm just about at the end of my rope,
But I can't give up tryin, I can't give up hope."

I was the shortest woman in the bar,
but you could always find me smiling up at you,
when you finally showed,
your scarf still wet from the snow, and you would wrap it
around my neck gently, laughing instead of a
regular hello.
We didn't drink much—
One whiskey for you and for me the smell of it on your breath,
your hand on my hip was all I needed.
Then we'd dance in place at the bar
sure no one noticed how close we were.
How could they know?
When we left, the door *whooshed* behind us, and
the dust of ages rose as if we were already ghosts.

II

Neon Signs

The Bull Rider

Katherine Hoerth

In Texas towns the tongues of men all taste
the same, like sour whiskey, dust between
the teeth. I think of this as neon lights
flicker above, my elbows on the bar.
A man sits down beside me, smells of sweat
and oil fields. He tucks his hands inside
his pockets, tells his story: he was once
a god on AstroTurf. I've heard it all
before, another song with steel guitar.
I lean in close and whisper in his ear:

I wanna ride a god right out this town.

He nods his head as though he understands.
I rise up from my stool and walk across
the boot scuffed floor. I mount the metal bull
that only drunken tourists ever try.
My fingers wrapped around the plastic horn,

I wave goodbye to his Aegean eyes;
the smell of smoke gives way to Padre breeze.
I kick my heels off, touch my naked toes
to froth. The metal bull between my legs
turns into flesh; the Coastal Bend recedes.

We ride all night to Crete, and I become
a woman even gods cannot resist.

The Archaeologist Dreams of Sleep

Kimberly Parish Davis

Gazing at the mirror in
the Honky Tonk Haven,
Weldon, the archaeologist from
Kalamazoo, saw a redneck gal—
the spitting image of Miz Blewit,
sourpuss terror of the middle school.

While learning to drive,
he'd squashed her flat,
and by fortune or miracle,
the adjustment to her ilium
and ischium gave her
a nebulous, haughty air all
the young honeys hankered after
as she hopped and skipped over
the saw-dusted dancefloor.

Now here she was in the Haven
of Honkey Tonk teaching the
young'uns to dance.
With a hop and a skip and

a *gliiiiide* to the side
a line of cowgirls scooted in time.
Weldon stared, wild-eyed,
longneck sweating in hand,
and he dreamed of sleep
as Miz Blewit heeled-
and-toed, nose in the air.

Chevy Pick-Up, Loaded

Ed Ruzicka

for Nicholas Zakis

Back while he lived on the Bayou, worked as a derrick hand,
Nick had a Chevy Silverado clean as a bullet.
When I hitched down there to find temp work
during breaks at L. S. U. we'd spin out
to the Hubba-Hubba Lounge where the juke box
always twanged out merciless, tear-drop crap.

Roughnecks just in from a two week shift could be seen
dancing with their cousin's wife at two in the afternoon.
That cousin now out for his own two week stint on a drilling floor
as this little Cajun queen lived it up for all she was worth
at the Hubba-Hubba Lounge mid-afternoon in Galliano, LA.

We just sipped suds until the phone rang and
the bar maid picked up. Then turned and asked,
"Anybody want a deck-hand job with Nolte Theriot"
Two hours later I'd be in a company van
headed to Sabine Pass, state of Texas.

Nick kept an English gent's black umbrella on the rack
in the rear cab window as a "fuck you very much"
to the rednecks that all set Winchesters there.
We'd wheel along the bayou counting gator heads,
flipping empties out the windows to let wind
sweep them back into the pick up's bed.

When he made the long trek to Baton Rouge,
Nick parked behind my rent shack so the repo man couldn't spy
his Silverado sitting hot, ticking down under the trill of crickets.
He'd pick Leonard Cohen songs on the front porch
or we'd hit the bars and disco clubs along College Drive
where Nick danced like some sort of electrified rooster.

There was no stopping that boy back then.
No trouble too big anywhere he went.
That Silverado must have finally got paid off
but it never did—no how, no way—run
down one single road headed into tomorrow.

Integration 1964

Dave Parsons

When James Brown's band
or most any Motown Group,
hits one of those ecstatically high
shrilling passionate sax notes, sweaty
Phil, tie loose, is swimming The Gator
on the gritty dance floor at Charlie's
Playhouse in after-hours' deep East Austin,
when it was the "bad part of town"
and we were like giddy young tourists
and I can taste wee-hour fried chicken
from nearby Ernie's Chicken Shack
and recall how we were always too high
to worry about the rumor of sleepy cooks
spitting into our honky customers' gravy
& mashed potatoes, we were flying our lives
through the sixties and we didn't have a clue
that we were like the Ugly Americans.

DALLIANCE

Ruth I. Healy

His voice, like a distant train whistle,
carries her from the drafty lantern-lit hall,
gives name to her fears
through his lonesome love songs.

He sees her in the shadows,
a wary field mouse,
with chestnut-colored hair,
a solitary creature from the fields.

He plays by ear.
He whispers into the mic words
meant only for her to hear.

The audience hushes,
turns around. He is the old fox
from the lair.

TRIPLE-TWO AT THE DANCE

Janet Lowery

a stretch villanelle

Between two triple steps and two walking steps
she loses track when dancing the Triple-Two
with the good-looking guy of the hazel eyes.

It's strange how, when following his lead, the count
trips her tongue and staggers her feet between
the *one-two-three, four-five-six,* and the *walk, walk*—

because with most men, she hits the *walk, walk,*
every time. This *agon* is cliché, she thinks,
but stares hard into the good-looking guy's hazel eyes

like a mesmerized child who's lost her place on a page.
For the length of a song, celestial accents chime,
more magical than two triple steps, two walking steps,

more ethereal than beats per minute, and she knows,
by these signs, she's formed a three-minute plan
for the hardcore-handsome man with the hazel-eyes.

Enter here: a remembrance of his history with others,
and of hers; of romances foiled quick-time, of shadow-plays,
and triple-timing fates, of walk-outs, of walking out:

in a flash, her toes grip the phantom slipper of glass
lost in the fairy tale book of her past. Last chords end
the enchantment of the Triple-Two. Two walking steps—
she's off the floor, no backward glance at his sea-green eyes.

PRICKLY PEAR

Katherine Hoerth

Like nymphs beneath the moon the women danced
to thumping beats, umbrella drinks held high.
They swayed their hips together, laughed because
they knew that men would watch them from afar
like lovesick gods and were more fun to spurn
than go home with. But Daphne, with her hair
in disarray, bare shoulders sparkling
with sweat and glitter, caught a young man's gaze—

his face was fresh, his dusty curls peeked out
from underneath a cowboy hat. He winked.

She rolled her green agave eyes, then gave
her back to him. But to his drunken eye,
in flight she was more fair. He slid his hand
across her chest and pulled her body close
as if a flower only grows for plucking.
Daphne felt her flesh begin to bud
like cacti blossoms, prickly spines emerging
to meet Apollo's tender fingertips.

Partner

Sarah Cortez

At the end of the bar—
the dark one looking
for no one, nursing his drink.
Sometime soon, I'll walk

up to him, slip one hand
into the crook of his elbow,
press my most luscious
self into his sturdy arm

and tell him he's got to
dance. With me. No excuses—
right now. He'll shift

off the stool—grinning
just enough to show he's
willing to be persuaded—
in the curving, cool blue,

beer-sign neon. We'll
move, as if we know
each other, into the swirling
lights of a mirrored

disco ball and its late-night
broken truths, all those faceted
bright lies—so hard to catch. One
night—on a weekend—real

soon. Real, real soon.

You Ain't the First Singed Hash Browns on My Plate

R. Gerry Fabian

You throw your arms around me
like we were separated lovers
finding one another after years apart.
Your alcoholic breath could melt metal.
The bartender looks at me
and I shrug as you attempt
to sit down in my lap.
I defeat that move by twisting you
onto the empty stool next to me.
"If you come home with me
I'll make you eggs and bacon."
The wedding band on your finger
suggests I will get cold pork shoulder.
And it would help just a little,
if I had any clue as to who you are.

Just Believe Her!

Alan Birkelbach

She swore she couldn't dance at all.
She tried to steer him clear.
She felt it safer all around
if she just drank her beer.

But he was brash and confident.
His skill would see them through!
I'm told the casts will come off in
another month or two.

Rodeo Exchange

karla k. morton

He would take me there
but refused the floor,
asking cowboys in ten-gallons
if they would dance with his wife.
It always seemed a trick question.

But given the green go,
one would always agree,
our orbit around the floor
like two cautious astronauts;

tiny bits of sawdust floating up;
my heart defying gravity
as I gave in
to strange arms.

Always,
he asked my name,
as if that's what made us human
in this alien world,

with its twirling,
silver-pocked ball;
its amber bottles
along the walls;

the hard K of my name
a galactic language
clicked
in great black space;

never again
so close to this chest;
never again
my hand on this shoulder;

this fresh showered skin—
a foreign sun
radiating through the gaps
of his taut pearl snaps.

BACK

Juleigh Howard-Hobson

The pedal steel notes resound like heartbeats,
And the gritty crunch of sawdust keeps you
Grounded in the moment. You take a seat
And look around, you've been gone too long to
Remember all the faces, but dancehall
Years are different and the smoky dusty
Memories suddenly come back through all
The lights and music. Above the rusty
Whines of fake bull riders, the juke box keeps
On playing songs you used to dance to when
The two of you were happy. So, you weep
In to your beer glass, looking now and then
To see if she appears, but the dance floor
Doesn't hold her, she's not there anymore.

I May Not Be Drunk, But I'll Get There

Herman Sutter

In the thickness of heat, no air, no sound,
weaving waves of foam (and the chair) keeps rising;
Hidalgo moves off the stool and stops, except the ground
keeps swaying, standing up, shivering down, rising
falling.

Juke box music floats in the beer light bleary as
a waitress lingering until someone sings or so Hidalgo
thinks. He sees four dancers dangling from the chandeliers;
he orders four more beers—golden stars rising,
falling.

Stumbling off the floor he staggers into the wings of a moon
moth gathering cigarette butts out of the glittering street rising
up to meet him stumbling. Concrete melting too soon
he pauses; the lamplight spooning midnight dripping rising
falling.

He tumbles into the lap of a puddle, bent over the black top
wet with sweat and damp with dew stuck shirt tight
rubbing the beer from his head rising into the night
golden stars rising into the emptiness that can't stop
falling.

Your Dancing Lessons Didn't Pay Off

J. J. Steinfeld

It's dime-a-dance night
an anachronism, surely
but there are other thoughts
tickling our desires
and a rumour the world
is going to reverse its orbit
a minute or two before midnight
whatever that will bring about
but for now it's ballroom bound
jostling the other dreamy dancers.

Inside the majestic ballroom
refurbished, painted a colour
from another time
your dancing lessons
didn't pay off
the half-crazed recluse
turns you down
says on another planet
you'd be fed to the bottom feeders
living halfway up the hidden mountain
and we spend the rest of the night
at the edge of the dance floor
trying to define our tastiness
to otherworldly creatures.

Little Heretic

Gerry LaFemina

One by One We Vanished

Another Absolut & cranberry juice. Another
broken evening, here near the landmarks of my adolescence:
Cherry Tavern, CBGB, Pyramid Club—They've all
disappeared into the collective memory of aging punks.
Exploited, Bad Brains, Minor Threat. Seems like

forever ago. Seems like forty-eight hours. Whatever
god I worshiped then (that girl in tight leather &
high heels, the cat who listened to my complaints),
I believed could save me from the brokerage firms &
Jesuits that seemed like the permanent forecast.

Kraut, the Circle Jerks, D.O.A. I
listened to drum barrage, screech & feedback thinking—
maybe—the holy spirit would fill me with distortion.
Nights like that—like this—lingered without end.
One by one we vanished into our

particular futures. Thus it seems so
quixotic to be back. Yet familiar, too. The bartender
returns with a fresh drink. He looks like
someone I knew those days; I recognize his laughter &
that tattoo on his arm of a mohawked teddy bear.

Understand, I stepped onto St. Marks earlier &
virtually every storefront had transformed although
westward still lay Broadway, Sixth Ave, the Hudson.
X, the Clash, Stiff Little Fingers. I listened to them,
yes, the songs like hymns I still remember: little

zealot that I once was. Little heretic.

WAITING FOR RESURRECTION

Leah Mueller

The Grande Ballroom in Detroit
dispensed music and sin seven days a week
for six years, until it ran out of money.

Even Ted Nugent sounded cogent
while describing his love for the place.
Alice Cooper, the MC5, Muddy Waters,
Cream, Led Zeppelin, the Who, BB King,
Frank Zappa, Iggy, the Grateful Dead
and countless other bands graced the stage.

The dressing room was open for groupies
and folks who wanted to tune Jeff Beck's guitar.
Kids got down behind the stage.
Their parents couldn't care less
what they were doing, or with whom.

A joyful, decadent time, before Detroit
collapsed into ruins, taking the Grande with it.

One frigid March afternoon in 2013,
I stood on the corner next to the Grande,
took cell phone photos of two friends
as they huddled beside the chain link fence.

They'd lived in Detroit their whole lives,
and had driven past the Grande
hundreds of times since its closure.
Still, they humored my need for documentation.

The two had been married
forty years, and were still in love,
but a little bored with each other.

He was an angry union guy on a vegan diet
who worked for the phone company,
and she had been fired ten years earlier
from her travel industry job.

They scowled as they leaned against
the crumbling bricks of the defunct ballroom,
the vivid pain of a Michigan winter
like angry red scratches across their faces.

Later, the woman showed me scars on her belly
from where her stomach had exploded
a few months beforehand. She almost died twice.

The scars were raw and purple, and
her skin bulged and sagged with their weight.

I stared, unable to comprehend.
Me: west coast girl, the one who escaped.
Seattle will collapse like Detroit, she said.
Everything on the west coast will one day
look exactly like the Grande Ballroom.

I laughed, said this was impossible.
A few months later, they stopped talking to me.

Of course, my friend was right, but I can't
be blamed for my refusal to believe.
Like those kids behind the stage,
I needed my illusions to last forever.

Now, when I look at the mirror
and the street corner, all I see is wreckage.

Perhaps if I run fast enough,
I can twist the knob in reverse,
go backwards and restore everything:

the ballroom, Detroit, this damaged land
that somehow allowed me to survive,
my lost friendships, and more than anything else,
all the times I turned away without listening.

Always

Anusha VR

As the music played
she twirled across the floor,
the audience watched in stunned silence.
It was thing of sheer beauty,
the intricate blend of melody and maneuvers.
Her piece ended,
a thunderous applause broke out.
Silence prevailed in the empty gymnasium.
The audience dissipated.
The janitor brushed away glimpses of an era gone by
as she hobbled across the room to mop the floors.
A phantom pain shot through her prosthetic leg
as she relived the night her car wrapped itself around a tree
like it was meeting a long lost lover.
Of all that she had lost,
her yearning to dance would always remain.

The Way We Danced Before I Became Another Ex in Texas

Laurie Kolp

In your arms, I was the only one
on the floor. We waltzed the night away,
two-stepped and jitterbugged to Brooks and Dunn.
In your arms, I was the only one.
You whispered in my ear as you spun
me around whiskey shots, George Strait.
In your arms, I was the only one.
On the floor, we waltzed the night away.

Dancing with a Cue Stick

George Drew

for Judith Kitchen, 1941-2014

Location is everything, say a small bar
in a smaller town, say Wells, New York,
not in a cavernous pool hall one
green-skinned table edging another,
leaving little room to maneuver a shot,
let alone for dancing with a cue stick.

So Wells it is, and was that August night
when she and Dooley—David, not Tom—
joined in, albeit encouraged by shots
of tequila or vodka, dances demanding
twosomes, after all, which gives each dancer
the confidence for dancing with a cue stick.

Confidence, then, is second on our list
of necessities, the third an appropriate dance.
Rock & Roll dancing?—forget about it.
Cue sticks aren't made for wild gyrations,
nor for body-numbing repetitions like
those rap music incites, or even reggae.

How about rumbas? Tangos? Too intricate,
too formal, both dances dressed in a tux.
Cue sticks call for care, and care means
slow and slower; means avoiding contusions,
scrapes or cuts; means avoiding knocks
against the head, against the hips, the knees.

Slow dancing of any kind is fine, the two
step even, but the best, the dance
just made for cue sticks, is the waltz,
and waltz is what she and Dooley did

that night in Wells, New York, in their hands
the cue sticks both supple and elegant.

Dooley faltered once, a brief misstep not
noticeable in any less perfect execution.
And her? Thirty years on and she has ended
just as she did that night—with grace,
each step measured, each taken without one
scratch, the dance done and the cue stick racked.

Death at the Dancehall

Janet Lowery

—for Edwin and Brenda

At first it seemed that no one knew him—the bulky guy
lying supine beneath a table over there in the gloom
on the carpet twenty feet from the deejay booth.

The deejay called the manager; the manager asked
over the loudspeaker if anyone knew CPR or owned
a defibrillator. The country music played on, and most

dancers kept two-stepping around the line of dance.
Among those that stepped off to help, a nurse knelt down
to compress the guy's chest, a man whose face, now gone grey

signaled me he'd already headed out to the other side.
She kept trying, anyway, to inspire his soul back into his flesh.
She was, she told us after they rolled the stretcher away,

the last woman to dance with the cowboy who wore a white hat
and kicked up his heels when he danced a polka,
a trait for which he was mocked by some and for which

he paid dearly that evening, but which endeared him
to the nurse. Sweating as she worked, her eyes wet with sorrow
for a man she'd known only briefly and who was dead

by the time she reached him, she said it was after
a fast polka she noticed him panting, but then
they'd parted ways—forever, as it turns out, unless,

perhaps, they run into each other in the afterlife. Later on,
a woman who worked the ER announced, "It's always
a fast polka that does it to the guys with heart conditions."

We all nodded our understanding, but, later on,
I wondered how we could ever know which guys
danced free of any conditions of the heart.

Two Dogs Howling at the Moon

Dave Parsons

for Rusty Wier 1944-2009

I will always remember the last time I saw you,
at your angel's, Tricia's crowded Plano townhouse

and how, after our four hours of harmoniously
catching-up on thirty some odd years of lost time,

I read you my poem *The Pride*, about that pack
we ran with—we thought we were lions, we were

more wolves or stray dogs—reliving those old stories
of growing up together wild in the enigmatic sixties

in South Austin, like our Tequila drinking contest
when I came home from the Marines, how I passed

out hearing you strumming to *Rave On*, learning
later, you had quickly followed me to the darkness

falling dead-drunk onto your beat up old guitar,
like some faithful warrior falling on his sword.

As our visiting ebbed, you played for me the second
of your three new songs, saying, "I'm still writing—

can't stop doing that one thing—we're like those two
old dogs in my song, David, we writers just keep barking

and howling at that ole' moon," your voice still
inimitably valved despite the chemo and the thousands

of songs poured out like manna to the many hungering
audiences of the nightlife you so loved and I remember

at that moment thinking how Li Po is said to have so
adored that great luminous orb that he perished, when

after a night of heavy drinking, he fell into the lake
attempting to embrace the dazzling antediluvian body, tumbling

head-long and alone into the deep ink of oblivion,
or perhaps, the masked reflections of pooling eternal light

and how you, after sailing through countless gigs
and seas of Agave, one complimentary shot at a time,

were now arduously floundering to make the best of each
of these last painfully clumsy egregious moments,

like you always have, with that distinctive dancing
twinkle in the weathered squint of those smiling blue

eyes, eyes still fully alive in my memory, still dancing—

I suppose every human passion holds within its core
the germ of something lethal to its being and yet,

somehow, interwoven with the potential of rapture.
Tonight the sheer linen curtains of my bedroom seem

to be tossed by the blurring energy of the moonlight
bouncing glowing stones across the dark water of our pool

as the ceiling fan circles in its perpetual waving orbits
and I can hear my daughter's tiny lap dog beneath

my small dinghy of a bed gnawing like memories
on a T-bone scrap from dinner, he is at that phase

where all the meat is flayed away and one can only
hear the sound of bone against bone as he is working

into a rhythm in his ceaseless mastication, creating
his own unique kind of wild, raw, self-satisfying music.

RESURRECTION MARY

Carolyn Kreiter-Foronda

In 1934 after a night of ballroom dancing, Mary was killed by a hit-and-run driver while hitchhiking a ride home. Buried in Resurrection Cemetery, this fabled Chicago ghost continues to make appearances.

Sir, I will not harm you.
All I need is a ride
on this lonely stretch of road
to a nearby ballroom.
Pearl-white gown billowing,
high-heeled shoes golden,
I'll waltz in your arms,
rise and fall to the sway
of the rhythm, fluid as silk.
Do not be frightened
if I dart around the room,
then vanish, virile as lake air.
Don't be frightened
if I suddenly reappear.
My beauty will stun you.
Come closer. Give me a ride
to O. Henry Ballroom, where
the ambiance is vibrant.
Hurry, the moon's alert.
It's midnight. Let's slip
into night's chill.
After dancing we'll
return to Archer Road
to the locked gates
of Resurrection Cemetery.
If I disappear, free
as a spirit, forgive me.
It's the anniversary of my death.

III

Neon Hearts

Standing on the Edge of the Roadhouse Charybdis

Alan Birkelbach

Don't you wish someone had told you
when you were fourteen
that your life was going
to come down to this evening?
It could be totally summarized
by you alone and standing at a wooden half-bar,
nursing an overpriced beer from an amber long-necked bottle,
watching people orbit in arm's reach.

When you drove up and parked on the gravel outside
the sound of life speeding by finally had noises:
the eighteen wheelers on the service road,
the motorcycles clustering like steroidal bees,
girls clustering and appraising—all laughter but no talk.

The speed of things, ah, the speed of things.
The way the dancing followed an orbit,
like a cyclone or whirlpool. You drove thirty plus years
to this evening and it's just spinning.

You noticed even in here that the music had partnered with time.
The songs ate up the minutes, and your years,
like somebody in there was an eternal hero
and was granted a pause.
And you were just a participant, a watcher, an extra, an unnamed sailor.

Maybe if you had a squarer jaw or dirtier boots.
But when it's timeless there's no questions.
You know, afterwards, if you choose to step outside
you will have grown a four inch beard.

Your hips might ache. You'll wish you had better memory.
You might have wished you had stayed.

Dancing Before

Lesley Clinton

On the midnight prairie, we found
a hall: Tejano and light radiating
from it like a western aurora. Inside,

red Solo cups of Lone Star, large families,
embroidery illuminating
boots and denim. In fact, all

illuminated: smiles, linoleum, fold-out
tables, starched shirts, starry black
hair brushed to the waist.

We danced there, before children,
to twelve-string fretwork decadent
as fireworks for two.

The singers—their scrollwork harmony
cactus-flower bright.
We saw our someday:

ageless smiles, summer
tracked in on kitchen linoleum, holidays
around fold-out tables, our daughter's

wispy hair, the messy joy
of it, our son's T-shirt covered
with ketchup, all of it. And we knew.

This twelve-string dance meant more—
more dancing,
denim, harmony—all of it

illuminated.

Zydeco Shindig

Dolores Comeaux

My mama grasps at the edge of her walker, swaying to zydeco,
Dipping and bouncing to the music at the *fais do do.*
A shabby shack of a dance hall, off a country road in Port Acres,
Seniors Cajun-dance to the squeak of the accordion,
Fiddle flying in rhythm to the spoon raking across a tin washboard.

Twinkling eyes and fleet-tapping feet of octogenarians and
Ninety-year-olds take nips of colas laced with a tad of whiskey—
Remembering earlier times as teens, erasing wrinkles and arthritis.
Time stands still as women dance with women who've outlived their men.
A lone survivor, an elderly gent, spreads himself thin dancing with 'em all.

Not "Saturday Night Live"—but Sunday afternoon—a stab at holding
    back thoughts of the hereafter.
Lively-aged limbs scoot dancers around in circles to "Jolie Blonde,"
Almost a Cajun anthem and one that most cut their teeth upon,
Along with sucking down gumbo, rice and beans—Cajun fare.
Swamp pop urges them *dansez, dansez* to chanky-chank music.

Misty eyed, I watch from the shadows as my mama is transformed
To her teen days of giggling, flirting, and having a fling.
The elderly gent asks me to dance and fills my ears with sweet nothings.
My mama warns he spins sugar for all the dainties he twirls on the floor,
Like a bee pollinating wilting flowers in hopes of a lasting evening bloom,
They wink, blink, smile, and blush in his arms to dance a fast step.
Laissez les bon temps rouler!
Let the good times roll!

Friday's Dance

Mike Schneider

Ribbon of horsehair scratches
stretched catgut while a banjo
rings an old-time rhythm—icy
winter, bony knuckle, rusted
plow. Sorrow murmurs in the wind
across broken strings of anybody's
heart until you can't say who's in tune

or out. Each word plays a part.
Never will there be another sunset
like tonight's, already melting into yesterday
as we take hands & circle, allemande left,
right, each of us a rhythm that can't go on
past midnight's iron chime, the royal
coachman, his pumpkin carriage waits.

Time with your neighbor will be brief
says the caller as he leads the dancers
through their steps. They shout for
More as Old Man Smith grins
& swings his belly in a dervish
whirl & busts out laughing for love
of nothing but a fiddle that sings
music to lift his dancing feet.

Road House on the Way to Cheyenne

Rick Campbell

After the kids had gone back to town
to rock and roll bars and bodies
like their own, the owner
would unplug the jukebox

and start his reel of favorite songs.
Popcorn was free and sometimes beer too.
And we'd listen. And we'd dance.
And he'd sit and tell us some story

we were privileged to know by heart
because all good stories are already ours.
After midnight, I'd look up at the bar,
the neon beer signs, a dead elk on the wall.

The fat man I imagined sad, long eyes
of a Basque sheepherder, would look at his wife
sleeping on the bar, head in her arms,
and then whisper to his dog—who waited for this moment—

wanna dance. Between bar and empty tables
he'd wrap his big arms around the mutt and sway
in the yellow light. They danced a slow circle,
no matter what the music said.

GUITAR AND MANDOLIN

Gerry LaFemina

In the music store the conversation's all string theory,
all guitar & mandolin, the occasional bass, &
always the next lick, the next riff, the next lament as if
so much of the ordinary were in a minor key.
That afternoon I bought a resonator
I swore I'd become a blues man,
howl the griefs that seemed for so long to reside
inside my spleen, sing them like Muddy or the Wolf,
guys on Chess & Alligator—
the sad news of the modern man, which isn't new
or modern nor limited to men. No surprise
I never learned those scales. All my life
I've swam the gulf between electric & ecstatic
with an overdrive pedal of rage to protect it all.
Everything is practice, everything routine:
pentatonic, tabulature, such small ways
to measure our measures, & after closing,
a pub where someone else, some lonely
woman with a plugged-in mandolin,
plays a few bars of songs brought over
from the old country, the saddest songs
she knows, & even though we understand
only the melodies listen to how everyone keeps time
drumming the tables, wanting to sing along.

Dress Code at the Dance Hall

Alan Birkelbach

Son, I'm afraid there's a dress code,
so let me just stop you right here.
You're flashy and pretty and playing the role—
but it's not just about what you wear.

Yes, I know that I'm only the greeter.
Here's some words before stepping inside.
A true cowboy's also a gentlemen.
Don't pretend you can saddle and ride.

That stage has seen Haggard and Willie
George Jones, Charlie Pride, Emmy Lou.
Your eyes don't show heartache. Your boots are uncreased.
I suspect that their songs weren't for you.

You say you're just here for the dancing.
You might know all the spins and the curls.
But I'd bet your cologne might just keep you alone
from these authentic rodeo girls.

But if you're dead-set on some stepping
and my speeching is leaving you cold,
just leave your hat there on the peg board.
I don't care if that band's solid gold.

There's nobody here that will take it.
There's no place that hat's gonna go.
Folks have done sized you up as you stood here.
They suspect that you're mostly just show.

Son, I'm afraid there's a dress code
and most of us here know our place.
These walls have a honky-tonk holy
so we try to show honor and grace.

We don't serve your single malt whiskey.
We don't serve cigars and what's more
we'd much be obliged if you wouldn't
be checking your texts on the floor.

Son, I'm afraid there's a dress code
and your voice is too loud for these walls.
It's making you seem that you're something
when you really ain't nothing at all.

There's no way to mask up what's inside you.
I don't care how those fancy jeans fit.
This hall's a good start if you're ready.
Learn humility, manners, and grit.

There's some people in line here behind you.
Their boots are still grimy with sand.
Son, I'm afraid there's a dress code.
Decide on the truth of your brand.

Here at Ransom's Saloon

George Drew

for Claude

Here at Ransom's Saloon there's a chandelier
made of deer antlers you can swing from,
and on one of the walls a wagon wheel you
can wedge yourself in and spin like mice.

Steak, chicken, seafood and burgers are
our specialties, and if liquor isn't quicker
enough to get your groove on there's the funkiest
little country band in all the Texas piney woods.

So let your hair down, all you buckaroos,
choose your poison, kick up your heels
with your honey and two-step the night away
yowling like a tomcat at the cheatin' moon;

then, when the dawn comes stumbling in,
pile into your pickups, sleep the day away
and come back for more; but for all our sakes,
Cowboys, please park your guns at the door.

Hard Wood

Jerry Bradley

Weeknights it's drinks on the patio,
line-dance lessons, and karaoke in the parlor,
but on Saturday night at the Round-Up
it's country all the way at the biggest
gay bar in the Metroplex.

Here the two-step dominates, and even
small men push their partners
in racetrack fashion around the floor.
Fast-fast slow-slow they go in 2/4 time,
counterclockwise, sliding the soles
of their pointy roachkillers across the parquet.

Beginners stick to the inner circle
so the experts can scoot by those
that stutter. Everyone wears a hat,
although one couple in trucker caps
wear theirs backwards to keep
their bills from bumping.

Impeccably they glide about
the crowded floor as if steered
by transponders on their wallet
chains or by echolocation.

Some dance the sweetheart side by side
and promenade the floor with the lead's
right hand draped across the follower's shoulders,
their left hands held in between
like couples in an engagement photo.

Others conduct each other about with a hand
in each other's pocket or cuddle side by side
like ice dancers. For guys used to leading,
the shadow step works well— especially
on George Strait songs and swing tunes.

On slower numbers they can hear
the stags flirting with bartenders,
the clack of pool balls rear-ending
one another, knowing at midnight
Cinderella will put on his golden slippers
when the music changes to top 40.

Bootstrap

Winston Derden

Pick yourself up off the floor.
Get your purse.
Get out the door.
Be good and gone before he's back.

Grab a tallboy at the 7/11 chest,
a handful of ice in a bandana,
a five and, "Keep the change,"
faster than the clerk can stare.

Half the tallboy in one swallow,
ice to eye so it won't swell,
maybe by the morning, the neck
and shoulder will be feeling well.

At the red light, take the highway,
drive out to the edge of town,
turn in at the Skyline Ballroom,
drink the last of that tallboy down.

Cabin light and rearview mirror,
blue mascara, rouge high up on the cheek.
Through the door, a smile for cover,
eyes attack the dancehall floor.

That old gray Stetson above the dancers,
the woman must be someone new.
Watch as they come closer.
Step out of your shoes.

Cut in when he twirls her.
Let surprise paint her face.
With one look, he knows
why I've stepped in to take her place.

Tears take out my eyeliner.
Rouge streaks the shoulder of his shirt.
He sees the bruise and the swelling.
I see his anger and his hurt.

Hold me like you did when I called you Daddy.
Dance me bare feet on top your boots.
Let me lean my head here on your shoulder.
Wrap me in love like you used to.

Hold on tight, little darling.
You know I'll never turn you loose.
You can tell me all about him later.
Just now, step down off my boots.

Move in time to the music. Don't follow me,
you'll always be behind the beat.
Stand up tall like I taught you.
Stop banging on my back with your shoes.

Hold me like you did when I called you Daddy,
wrap me in a love that doesn't hurt,
whisper those words that calm and soothe.
Turn me slow and gentle, help me turn and face the truth.

6 A.M. OUTSIDE THE DANCE HALL

John Grey

The dancers slip away
leaving only the dew,
crystal on the pistil.
The steps are empty.
Even the younger faces
are too old to stay.
The lily's being gilded
by nothing but sun on water,
a drip to the end of music,
a patter on a silken lip
as the drummer packs his kit.
The wild life's been pumped
out of the hall
The wax flowers died
in deference to the real thing.
All the beer that ever flushed a face,
buzzed a brain,
pried loose the muscles in the knees,
rests in the sleeping stomach
or bubbles through the sewage pipes.
Only a flower is left
to let down its silky guard,
ripple with the dawn's affection.

EMPTIES

Gerry LaFemina

I still enjoy these nights—a storm forming to the east
and me with a porch seat. I still forget sometimes
that I don't need to leave at ten for the club
and the inevitable clash with some drunk
whose mouth was louder than the crash

of guitars and bass and cymbals. I still like my music loud,
although some nights I miss the brash pogo stick
of conversation with waitresses and regulars. And after I wheeled out

the trash, after the empties had been stacked
and the cooler filled with Millers, I'd sit with a twelve-ounce, my body unstable
and stuttering on a bar stool as I stared through the picture window,

like a failed clairvoyant. And of two friends I worked with then?
Who knows.

Chris Lee with his ivy of violet braids, the tattoo of a teddy bear
clutching a machine gun on his arm, and his exhibitionist fables,
always another woman; and the other Chris

for whom fear was a racist cop, enjoyed his food and his dope almost
as much as he loved to laugh— a deep eruption
emanating from his bone girders outward to his 280 pound girth.

I still see them some nights, the same way
I'd see their reflections after closing,
standing behind me at the star-fighter game,
and beyond them the bartender vending one last illegal shot to the soundman.
A band breaking down in the distance.

The rain still fills the potholes on Michigan Ave.,
the wet tarmac stretching the stolen light of street lamps the length of a block.
I still like my music loud—
and in bars all over America punk rock kids are plugging Stratocasters
into patchwork amplifiers. It makes me happy

this rain, but it reminds me of big Chris who stripped his shirt
one night and stood in the street singing
what? I couldn't hear. He started soaping himself
with the night. Rain filled his near-empty bottle
and soon he sipped big and frowned as if suddenly he knew

his future and it frightened him. Then he ran off,
his body slick and brilliant with perspiration and rain
so he almost shone like obsidian

while Chris Lee and I stayed by the window, our hair shivering. Shit,
he said, not as an expletive but as a defeated act
of vocabulary—his inability to choose a different word.

I still like my music loud. I still like storms like this one,
all the rain close to home, all the lightning
miles away, so there's no thunder, no sounds at all

but for the sanitizing drum roll of the shower
on the roof and the tread of loud, individual drops which strike the soft earth,
setting what it holds free.

Contributor Bios

Alan Birkelbach, a Texas native, is the 2005 Texas State Poet Laureate. He is a member of the Texas Institute of Letters and the Academy of American Poets. He was an lndie Book Award Finalist twice. He is also a winner of a Spur Award for Best Western Poem from the Western Writers of America. He has 11 books of poetry.

Jerry Bradley, a member of the Texas Institute of Letters, is University Professor of English and the Leland Best Distinguished Faculty Fellow at Lamar University. He is the author of eight books and has published in *New England Review, Modern Poetry Studies, Poetry Magazine*, and *Southern Humanities Review*. He lives in Beaumont, Texas.

Rick Campbell is a poet and essayist living on Alligator Point, Florida. His latest collection of poems is *Gunshot, Peacock, Dog*. He's published five other poetry books as well as poems and essays in numerous journals including *The Georgia Review, Fourth River, Kestrel*, and *New Madrid*. He teaches in the Sierra Nevada College MFA Program.

Lesley Clinton has published poems in *Mezzo Cammin*, the *2017 Texas Poetry Calendar*, Houston Poetry Fest anthologies, *Sakura Review, Euphony Journal, Frogpond Journal, The Heron's Nest, Literary Mama*, and others. Her poems have won awards from the Poetry Society of Texas. She teaches English and co-moderates Inkwell Creative Writing Club at Strake Jesuit College Preparatory.

Christine Cock says, "This poem arose from a prompt from our Brooksville Writers' Group. Originally, we were asked to either meet an actor or be an actor. Matt Dillon was my true love when I was a little girl, so that is who I elected to write about."

Dolores Comeaux was born into a Cajun French family from Southwest Louisiana, was named after actress Dolores Del Rio (who played the lead in the movie, Evangeline), and cut her baby teeth on gumbo; thus, her addiction to all things Cajun. Her newest series features critters indigenous to the area who, through their zany antics, tell a tale of loss to the Louisiana wetlands. *Crittersville Capers: A Double-Dog Dare* is followed by *Crittersville Capers: Bayou Brouhaha*, the second in the series. In years past, Dolores was a reporter for a daily newspaper in Texas and wrote humorous columns. She earned a doctorate in psychology to teach. Her hobbies are writing and "clowning around." Now retired, she makes her home in Arizona with family. A member of Professional Writers of Arizona, she has published works in *Best Poetry* by AZ Writers and *Best Short Stories Book One* by AZ Writers.

Sarah Cortez is a Fellow of the Dallas Institute of Humanities and Culture and of the Virginia Center of the Creative Arts. Her poems, short stories, essays, book reviews, etc. have appeared in the nation's most respected newspapers and journals. Winner of the PEN Literary Award in Poetry, she has won numerous awards across the U.S. and internationally.

Kimberly Parish Davis spent a number of years as assistant to the director at Texas Review Press. She has published fiction, nonfiction and poetry in various journals and magazines, most recently, *FLAR, The Helix*, and *The Caribbean Writer*. She is the director of Madville Publishing, and she holds an MFA in Creative Writing, Editing, and Publishing from Sam Houston State University.

Winston Derden is a poet and fiction writer residing in Houston. He owns him a coupla Stetsons and some ostrich boots. His poetry publications include *New Texas, Blue Collar Review, Big River Poetry Review, Illya's Honey, Barbaric Yawp, 'Merica Magazine, Soft Cartel, Down in the Dirt, Plum Tree Tavern*, and numerous anthologies. He earned a BA and MA at the University of Texas, Austin.

George Drew is the author of seven poetry collections, most recently *Pastoral Habits: New and Selected Poems, Down & Dirty* and *The View from Jackass Hill*, winner of the 2010 X.J. Kennedy Poetry Prize, all from Texas Review Press. His eighth, *Fancy's Orphan*, appeared in 2017, Tiger Bark Press.

R. Gerry Fabian is a retired English instructor. He has been publishing poetry since 1972 in various poetry magazines. His has published three novels, *Memphis Masquerade, Getting Lucky (The Story)*, and *Seventh Sense*, and one poetry collection, *Parallels*. His second poetry collection, *Coming Out of the Atlantic*, is slated for publication in 2019.

John Grey is an Australian poet, US resident. His work was recently published in the *Homestead Review, Harpur Palate* and *Columbia Review* with work upcoming in the *Roanoke Review*, the *Hawaii Review* and *North Dakota Quarterly*.

Karen Head is the author of *Lost on Purpose* (Iris Press, forthcoming 2019), *Sassing* (WordTech Press, 2009), *My Paris Year* (All Nations Press, 2009) and *Shadow Boxes* (All Nations Press, 2003). Along with three colleagues, she published an anthology of occasional verse, *On Occasion: Four Poets, One Year* (Poetry Atlanta Press, 2014). She also creates digital poetry. She is an Associate Professor at Georgia Tech, and is the Editor of *Atlanta Review.*

Ruth I. Healy grew up in the hills of Pennsylvania, running barefoot, playing in the woods, and climbing trees, her favorite hideaways for reading mysteries. For the past couple decades, she has been a middle school English teacher in rural Connecticut. Teaching middle schoolers to appreciate literature sparked her own passion for reading and writing poetry.

Katherine Hoerth is the author of three poetry collections: *The Lost Chronicles of Slue Foot Sue* (Angelina River Press, 2018), *Goddess Wears Cowboy Boots* (Lamar University Literary Press, 2014), and *The Garden Uprooted* (Slough Press, 2012). She is the 2015 recipient of the Helen C. Smith Prize for the best book of poetry in Texas, and she is a member of the Texas Institute of Letters.

Juleigh Howard-Hobson's poetry has appeared in *Abridged, The Ginger Collect, The Non-Binary Review, The Lyric, Able Muse, Poem, Revised* (Marion Street Press), and other places. Nominations include "Best of the Net," The Pushcart Prize and The Rhysling Award. Her most recent book is *Our Otherworld* (Red Salon).

Laurie Kolp's poems have recently appeared in the *Southern Poetry Anthology VIII: Texas, Stirring, Whale Road Review, concis, Up the Staircase*, and more. Her poetry books include the full-length *Upon the Blue Couch* and chapbook *Hello, It's Your Mother*. An avid runner and lover of nature, Laurie lives in Beaumont with her husband, three children, and two dogs.

Lisa Naomi Konigsberg says, "This poem came out of a 45-year relationship with a man, a city (Philadelphia), and poetry. All three of those things have fueled my writing at different times, but more often, I am wedded to the belief that my poems will save me." She has a chapbook titled, *Invisible Histories*, from Spruce Alley Press, 2015.

Carolyn Kreiter -Foronda served as Poet Laureate of Virginia from 2006-2008. She has coedited three anthologies and published eight books of poetry, including *The Embrace*, winner of the Art in Literature: The Mary Lynn Kotz Award. Her poems appear in *Nimrod, Prairie Schooner, Mid-American Review, Best of Literary Journals, Poet Lore, World Poetry Yearbook*, and others. Her book, *These Flecks of Color: New and Selected Poems* was released in 2018.

Gerry LaFemina is the author of 8 collections of poetry, most recently *The Story of Ash* (2018, Anhinga Press) and 3 collections of prose poetry. His textbook, *Compo sing Poetry: A guide to writing Poems and Thinking Lyrically* was released by Kendall Hunt. He teaches at Frostburg State University and serves as a mentor in the Carlow University MFA program.

Janet Lowery's poetry has been published in journals such as *Poetry East, Greensboro Review, Concho River Review*, and in anthologies such as *Untameable City* and *Improbable Worlds* from Mutabilis Press; *Texas in Poetry 2* (TCU Press); *Who Are the Rich and Where Do They Live?* (from *Poetry East* 2000); *Far Out: Poems of the '60s*, and in *Southern Poetry Anthology: Volume VIII: Texas*. A chapbook of her poetry, *Thin Dimes*, was published by Wings Press in the 1990s. A collection of poetry from her trilogy of plays calling attention to human trafficking *Traffic in Women I, II, III* was published by Odonata House in 2008. Her latest play, *A Heroine Free Summer* was produced by Mildred's Umbrella Theater Company in Houston, 2017.

Philip "Pj" Metz is a high school English teacher from Orlando, Florida. He has been a poet since he first performed at an open mic in Busan, South Korea in 2017. He's been previously published in Angle Magazine, a South Korean online magazine, Starfall Sea, an Orlando based literary magazine, and has had his work performed at Pipsqueak Collective's inaugural Squeakfest, a performance of local author's works. He is active in Orlando's arts scene through music, theater, and poetry, and is thankful for every opportunity to share his work with anyone willing to listen.

Award winning 2010 Texas Poet Laureate **karla k. morton** has twelve poetry collections. A Wrangler Award Winner, Indie National Book Award winner, Betsy Colquitt award winner, and E2C Grant recipient, she's widely published and seeks out every dancehall she can across the US while on her "Words of Preservation: Poets Laureate National Parks Tour."

Leah Mueller is the author of two chapbooks and four books. Her latest book, a memoir entitled *Bastard of a Poet* was published by Alien Buddha Press in June 2018. Leah's work appears or is forthcoming in *Blunderbuss, The Spectacle, Outlook Springs, Mojave River Review, Drunk Monkeys, Atticus Review, Your Impossible Voice, Wolfpack Press*, and other publications.

Dave Parsons, 2011 Texas State Poet Laureate, is a recipient of an NEH Dante Fellowship to SUNY Geneseo, the French-American Legation Poetry Prize, and the Baskerville

Publisher's Prize. He was inducted into The Texas Institute of Letters in 2009. Parsons has published seven poetry collections. His latest are *Reaching for Longer Water* and *Far Out Poems of the 60's*, co-edited with Wendy Barker. He is founder and co-director of Montgomery County Literary Arts Council Writers In Performance Series.

Gianna Russo is the author of *Moonflower*, winner of a Florida Book Award. Pushcart Prize nominee, she has had publications in *Green Mountains Review*, *The Sun*, *Poet Lore*, *The MacGuffin*, *Tampa Review*, *Crab Orchard Review*, *Florida Review* and *Water Stone*, among others. She is founding editor of the poetry chapbook publisher YellowJacket Press. She holds an MFA in Poetry from The University of Tampa and is Assistant Professor of English and Creative Writing at Saint Leo University.

Ed Ruzicka has published one full length volume, *Engines of Belief*. His poems have appeared in the *Atlanta Review*, *Rattle*, the *New Millennium Review*, and *Chicago Literati*, as well as other literary journals and anthologies. Ed lives in Baton Rouge, LA and is an occupational therapist.

Mike Schneider has published in many journals, including *Notre Dame Review*, *New Ohio Review* and *Poetry*. In 2012 he received The Florida Review Editors Award in Poetry. In 2017 he won the Robert Phillips Prize from Texas Review Press, which published his second chapbook, *How Many Faces Do You Have?*

Luanne Smith lives in New Jersey and works in Pennsylvania, but she is a born Kentuckian. She is an Associate Professor at West Chester University outside of Philadelphia where she has taught creative writing and film for nearly 30 years. Her work, usually short fiction, has appeared in *Puerto del Sol*, *The Oxford Review*, *The Texas Review* and other literary journals. This is her second poetry publication. Her first was about Koko, the gorilla.

Canadian poet/fiction writer/playwright **J. J. Steinfeld** lives on Prince Edward Island, where he is patiently waiting for Godot's arrival and a phone call from Kafka. While waiting, he has published 19 books, including *Identity Dreams and Memory Sounds* (Poetry, Ekstasis Editions, 2014), *Madhouses in Heaven, Castles in Hell* (Stories, Ekstasis Editions, 2015), *An Unauthorized Biography of Being* (Stories, Ekstasis Editions, 2016), *Absurdity, Woe Is Me, Glory Be* (Poetry, Guernica Editions, 2017), and *A Visit to the Kafka Café* (Poetry, Ekstasis Editions, 2018).

Herman Sutter is a school librarian living in Houston, Texas with his wife, three daughters, four cats, a fish and nineteen turtles. His poems have appeared in *Touchstone*, *blonde on blonde, i.e.*, *The Northern Review*, and *St. Anthony Messenger*, among others. In 1982 his narrative poem "Constance" received the Innisfree prize for poetry. His chapbook *The World Before Grace* (1992), was the inaugural volume in the Texas Poetry Sampler series from Wings Press.

Anusha VR is a CA, CS, author and spoken word poet residing in India. She is the author of three chapbooks—*Potpourri*, *Rotting Fruit* and *The Voices of Immigrants*. Her work has also appeared in over forty anthologies.